ACCA

Advanced Audit and Assurance (AAA)

Pocket Notes

British library cataloguing-in-publication data

A catalogue record for this book is available from the British Library.

Published by:
Kaplan Publishing UK
Unit 2 The Business Centre
Molly Millars Lane
Wokingham
Berkshire
RG41 2QZ

ISBN 978-1-78740-652-0

Printed and bound in Great Britain.

Acknowledgements

This Product includes propriety content of the International Accounting Standards Board which is overseen by the IFRS Foundation, and is used with the express permission of the IFRS Foundation under licence. All rights reserved. No part of this publication may be reproduced, stored in a retrieval system, or transmitted in any form or by any means, electronic, mechanical, photocopying, recording, or otherwise, without prior written permission of Kaplan Publishing and the IFRS Foundation.

Trade Marks

Contents

This document references IFRS® Standards and IAS® Standards, which are authored by the International Accounting Standards Board (the Board), and published in the 2019 IFRS Standards Red Book.

The content and style of the exam

	Number of marks
Section A – one question	
Planning, risk assessment, gathering evidence, ethical and professional considerations	46
Professional marks	4
	50
Section B – two questions	
Completion, review and reporting	25
Any area of the syllabus from:	25
• Regulatory environment	
• Ethical and professional considerations	
• Quality control and practice management	
• Planning and conducting an audit of historical information	
• Other assignments	
	100

All questions are compulsory
Current issues can be examined in any part of the exam

Aim of the exam

To ensure that candidates can exercise judgement and apply techniques in the analysis of matters relating to the provision of audit and assurance services and can evaluate and comment on current practices and developments.

The keys to success

- Answer all requirements to each question attempted
- Be strict with your time. REMEMBER: 1.8 minutes per mark (after reading time).
- There is very little scope for note learned knowledge: you MUST apply your knowledge to the specific circumstances of the scenario.
- Take your time to read and understand the full question requirement before reading the scenario.

Quality and accuracy are of the utmost importance to us so if you spot an error in any of our products, please send an email to mykaplanreporting@kaplan.com with full details, or follow the link to the feedback form in MyKaplan.

Our Quality Co-ordinator will work with our technical team to verify the error and take action to ensure it is corrected in future editions.

chapter

1

Regulatory environment

In this chapter

- Main sources of regulation.
- Public oversight and corporate governance.
- Audit committees.

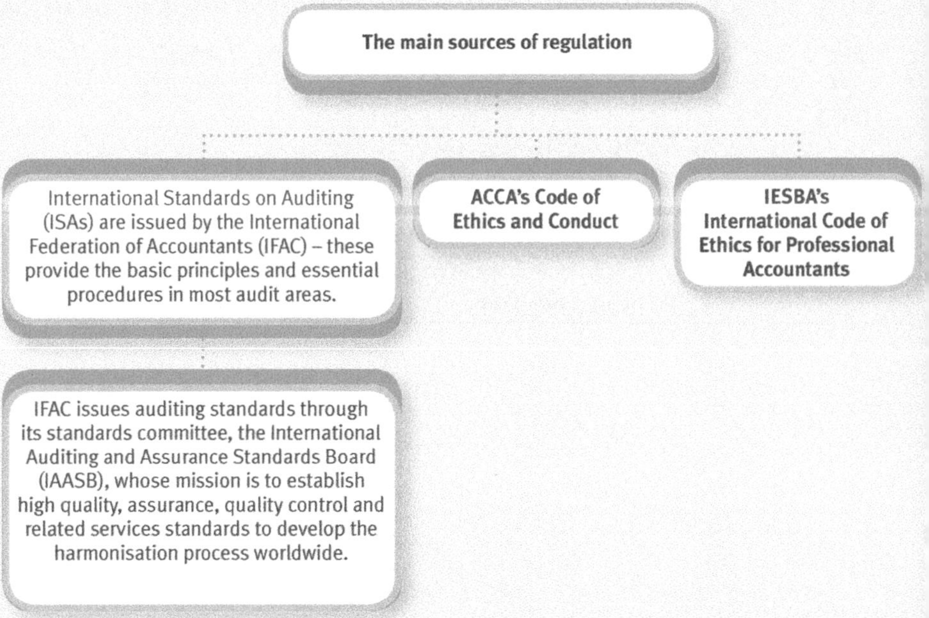

The main sources of regulation

International Standards on Auditing (ISAs) are issued by the International Federation of Accountants (IFAC) – these provide the basic principles and essential procedures in most audit areas.

ACCA's Code of Ethics and Conduct

IESBA's International Code of Ethics for Professional Accountants

IFAC issues auditing standards through its standards committee, the International Auditing and Assurance Standards Board (IAASB), whose mission is to establish high quality, assurance, quality control and related services standards to develop the harmonisation process worldwide.

Public oversight and corporate governance

Corporate governance is about ensuring that public companies are:

- managed effectively
- for the benefit of the company and its shareholders.

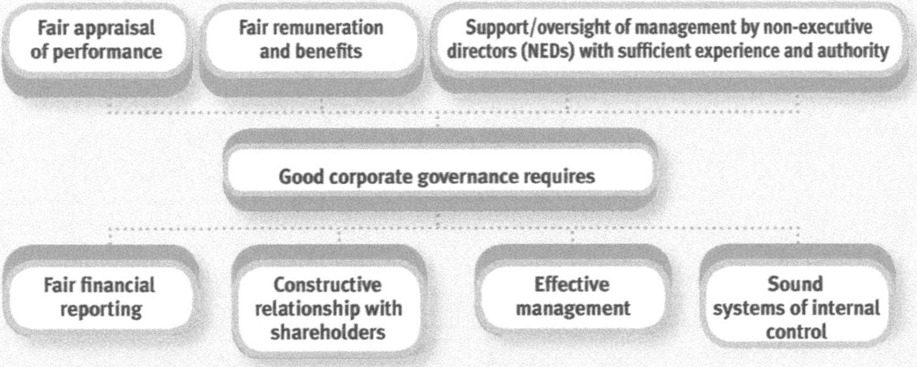

Fair appraisal of performance

Fair remuneration and benefits

Support/oversight of management by non-executive directors (NEDs) with sufficient experience and authority

Good corporate governance requires

Fair financial reporting

Constructive relationship with shareholders

Effective management

Sound systems of internal control

Good corporate governance can be enforced:

- by law – e.g The Sarbanes-Oxley Act, USA
- by agreement through codes of best practice – e.g. UK Corporate Governance Code, or
- through a combination of the two.

Corporate governance in action

Board leadership and company pupose

- Effective board leadership
- Promote long-term sustainable success
- Directors should lead by example

Division of responsibilities

- Independent chair leads the board
- CEO and chair should be 2 individuals
- Board should be balanced
- Half the board should be independent

Composition, succession and evaluation

- Board appointments made by Nomination committee (majority INEDs)
- Appointments based on merit – best person for the job
- Combination of skills and experience
- Annual re-election of all directors
- Chair must be replaced after 9 years

Audit, risk and internal control

- Board should ensure independence of IA and EA functions
- Board should manage risks and oversee internal controls
- Audit committee must be established (min 3 INEDs)
- Chair should not be a member of audit committee
- At least one member with recent and relevant experience

Remuneration

- Remuneration set by Remuneration committee (min 3 INEDs)
- Remuneration should promote long-term sustainable success
- Policy for setting remuneration should be formal and transparent
- No director should be involved in setting his own pay
- Board chair can only be a member of RC if independent on appointment
- Workforce pay should be considered when setting exec pay
- NEDs paid according to time commitments and responsibilities

Audit committees

Objectives

- Increase public confidence in credibility and objectivity of published financial info.
- Assist directors in meeting their responsibilities in respect of financial reporting.
- Strengthen the independence of the external auditor.

Advantages:

- Improve quality of management accounting.
- Improved communication between directors, external auditors and management.
- Avoids conflicts between auditors and management.

Main functions include:

- Review of company internal control procedures.
- Review of internal audit function.
- Review of external auditors results to ensure audit has been carried out efficiently, effectively and independently.
- Recommending remuneration and nomination of auditors.
- Reviewing requirements satisfied under UK Corporate Governance Code.

Disadvantages:

- Fear purpose to "catch out" management .
- Overburdening of non-executive directors.
- May lead to "two-tier" board.
- Costly.

Exam focus

To practise the basics use the following test your understandings (TYUs) Study Text: Chapter 1:

- TYU 1 'Becher'

chapter

2

Money laundering

In this chapter

- Money laundering.

Money laundering

Definition

Money laundering: process by which criminals attempt to conceal the true origin and ownership of the proceeds generated by illegal means.

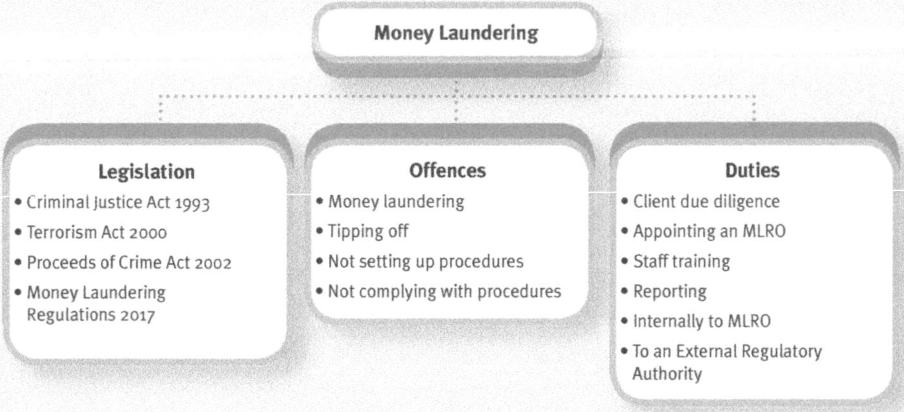

Money Laundering

Legislation

- Criminal Justice Act 1993
- Terrorism Act 2000
- Proceeds of Crime Act 2002
- Money Laundering Regulations 2017

Offences

- Money laundering
- Tipping off
- Not setting up procedures
- Not complying with procedures

Duties

- Client due diligence
- Appointing an MLRO
- Staff training
- Reporting
- Internally to MLRO
- To an External Regulatory Authority

Client identification

- Client identification and verification is a key component of client due diligence:

Typical Client Identification Procedures

For an individual

Establish the client's full name and address.

Examine:

- utility bills
- driving licence
- passport.

For a company

Obtain copies of the following from the registrar:

- certificate of incorporation
- register of directors
- register of members/ shareholders
- registered address.

For a trust

Examine trust deed.

Ascertain:

- identities of trustees and beneficiaries
- the purpose of the trust
- sources of funding.

Exam focus

Exam kit questions in this area:

- Thomasson & Co
- Vizsla
- Lark & Co

chapter

3

Code of ethics and conduct

In this chapter

- Fundamental principles.
- Threats & safeguards.
- Confidentiality.
- Conflicts of interest.

Fundamental principles

The code identifies five fundamental principles in professional conduct.

- **Integrity:** Members should be straightforward and honest in all professional and business relationships.
- **Objectivity:** Members should not allow bias, conflicts of interest or undue influence of others to override professional or business judgements.
- **Professional competence and due care:** Members have a continuing duty to maintain professional knowledge and skill to ensure that clients receive competent professional service based on current developments in practice, legislation and techniques. Members should act diligently and in accordance with applicable technical and professional standards when providing professional services.
- **Confidentiality:** Members should respect the confidentiality of information acquired as a result of professional and business relationships and should not disclose any such information to third parties without proper and specific authority or unless there is a legal or professional right or duty to disclose.
- **Professional behaviour:** Members should comply with relevant laws and regulations and should avoid any action that discredits the profession.

Threats & safeguards

Members are required to apply the conceptual framework to identify threats to compliance with the fundamental principles, to evaluate their significance and, if such threats are other than clearly insignificant, to apply safeguards to eliminate them or reduce them to an acceptable level such that compliance with the fundamental principles is not compromised.

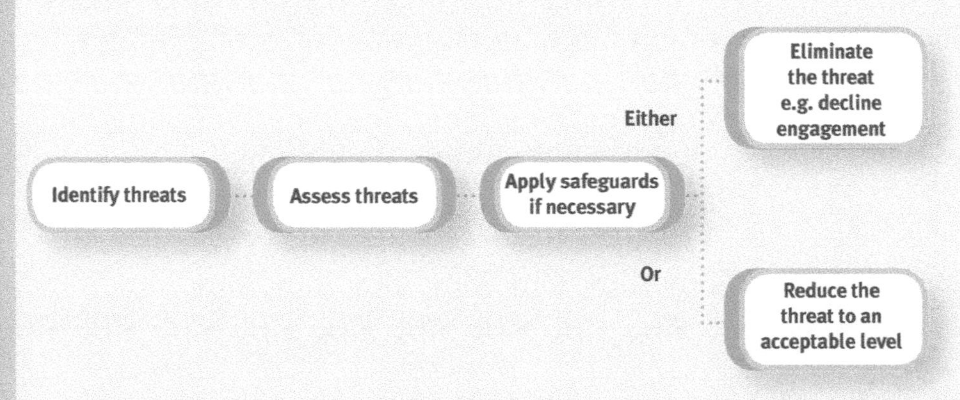

To evaluate the significance, consider materiality of the matter, the seniority of the people involved, etc.

Threats

The ACCA Code sets out the broad range of categories that the threats fall into:

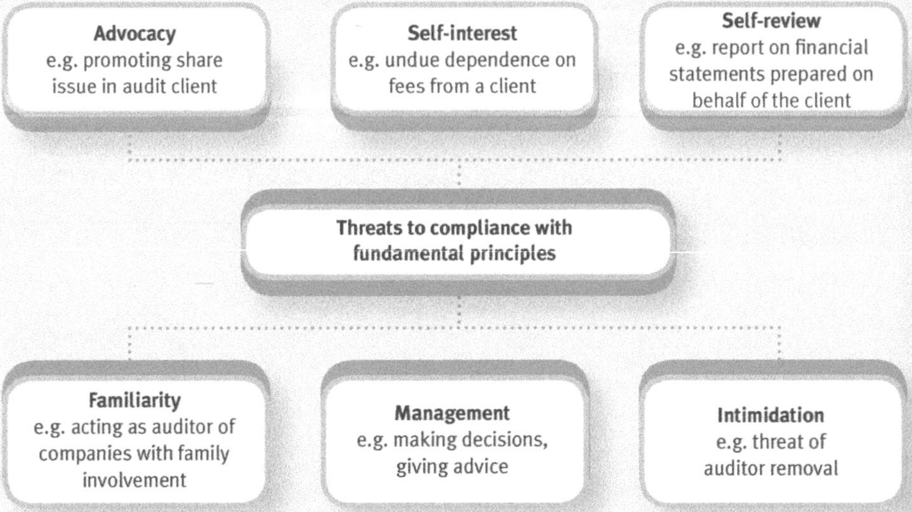

Advocacy
e.g. promoting share issue in audit client

Self-interest
e.g. undue dependence on fees from a client

Self-review
e.g. report on financial statements prepared on behalf of the client

Threats to compliance with fundamental principles

Familiarity
e.g. acting as auditor of companies with family involvement

Management
e.g. making decisions, giving advice

Intimidation
e.g. threat of auditor removal

Confidentiality

Members acquiring information in the course of their professional work should not disclose it to third parties unless:

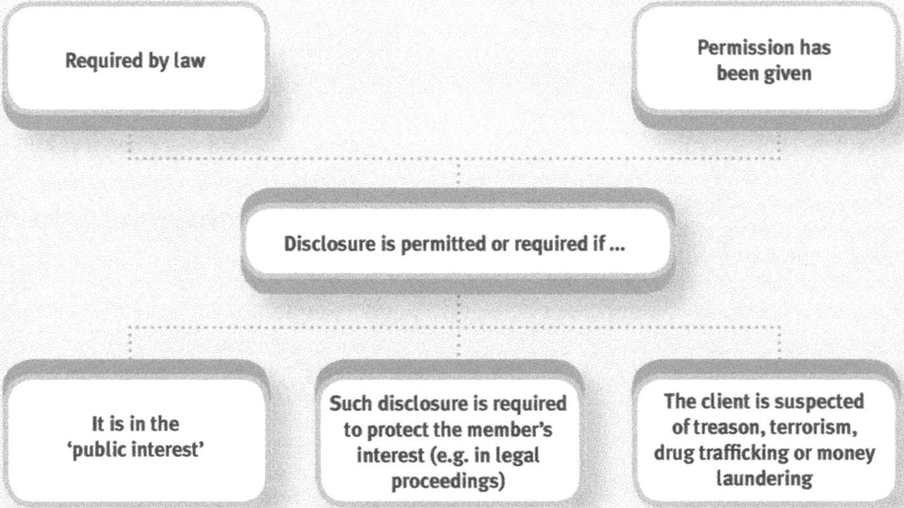

Required by law

Permission has been given

Disclosure is permitted or required if ...

It is in the 'public interest'

Such disclosure is required to protect the member's interest (e.g. in legal proceedings)

The client is suspected of treason, terrorism, drug trafficking or money laundering

Conflicts of interest

Arise where an auditor acts for both a client company and for a competitor company of the client. This situation is acceptable where appropriate safeguards are implemented.

The firm must notify all affected clients of the conflict and obtain their consent to act.

Additional safeguards must be implemented.

Where the acceptance/continuance of an engagement would, despite safeguards, materially prejudice the interests of any clients, the appointment should not be accepted/continued, or one of the appointments should be discontinued.

Safeguards against conflicts of interest

- Regular review of safeguards by an independent senior partner/ compliance officer
- Use of different partners and teams of staff for different engagements
- Information Barriers – to prevent leakage of confidential information between different years and sections within the firm
- Advising at least one or all clients to seek additional advice (last resort)

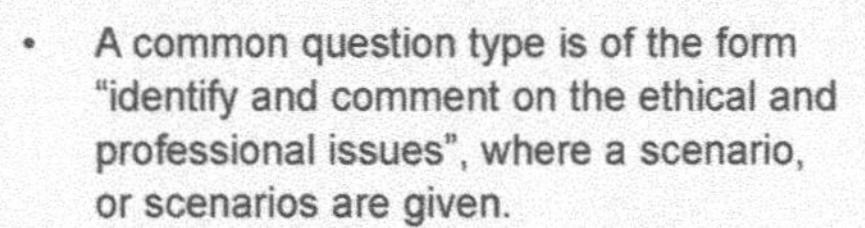

Exam focus

- A common question type is of the form "identify and comment on the ethical and professional issues", where a scenario, or scenarios are given.
- You should consider and explain all potential threats within a scenario, identify actions that should be taken in coming to conclusions about the seriousness of the threats, propose potential safeguards and ultimately what actions should be taken.
- You **must** expand on all of these areas – simply identifying that there is a threat to independence will not get you any marks!
- Always look at how many marks are available for each part of a scenario – use it as a guide to how many points you need to cover within your answer.

Exam focus

Exam kit questions in this area:

- Ryder Group
- Eagle Group
- Bassett Group
- Coram & Co
- Thomasson & Co
- Adams Group
- Vancouver Group
- Dali
- Ted
- Grohl
- CS Group
- Rope
- Cheetah
- Macau & Co

chapter

4

Professional responsibilities and liabilities

In this chapter

- Laws and regulations in an audit of financial statements.
- Fraud and error.
- Auditor liability.
- Expectation gap.

Laws and regulations in an audit of financial statements

ISA 250 Consideration of Laws and Regulations in an Audit of Financial Statements covers illegal acts by the client company.

Director's responsibilities	Auditor's responsibilities
• To ensure the entity complies with relevant laws and regulations. • To establish effective arrangements for preventing and detecting non-compliance.	• To obtain reasonable assurance that the financial statements, are free from material misstatement. • To obtain sufficient, appropriate evidence regarding compliance with those laws and regulations generally recognised to have a direct effect on the determination of material amounts and disclosures in the financial statements. • To perform specified audit procedures to help identify instances of non compliance that may have a material impact on the financial statements. • To respond appropriately if non compliance is identified (or suspected).

Procedures required by ISA 250:

- Obtain a general understanding of the legal and regulatory framework and of how the entity is compliant
- Inspecting correspondence with relevant licensing or regulatory authorities
- Enquiring of the management as to whether the entity is in compliance with such laws and regulations
- Consider the results of other audit procedures
- Obtaining written confirmation from directors that they have disclosed all events which involve possible non compliance.

Reporting non-compliance

To management and those charged with governance

To shareholders
Consider implication on audit opinion.

To third parties
Need to bear in mind duty of confidentiality but also duty to public interest.

Fraud and error

ISA 240 The Auditor's Responsibility Relating to Fraud in an Audit of Financial Statements

Fraud = intentional acts of deception

(May involve falsification of documents and records, misappropriation of assets, or misapplication of accounting policies)

Error = unintentional misapplication

Of accounting policies, oversights or misinterpretations

Management primarily responsible for the prevention and detection of fraud and error through the implementation and operation of adequate accounting and internal control systems

Auditor responsibilities

- Obtain reasonable assurance that the financial statements, taken as a whole, are free from material misstatement, whether caused by fraud or error.
- Maintain an attitude of professional scepticism.
- Identify and assess the risks of material misstatement due to fraud.

Fraud risk assessment procedures

- Engagement teams should discuss the risk of fraud.
- Consider the results of controls tests and analytical procedures.
- Enquire of client how they assess, and respond to, fraud risk.
- Enquire if client is aware of actual or suspected fraud.
- Consider incentives to commit fraud e.g. performance related bonuses.

Audit procedures

- Review year-end journals and adjustments.
- Review accounting estimates and areas of management judgment.
- Review transactions outside the normal course of business.
- Obtain written representation from management.

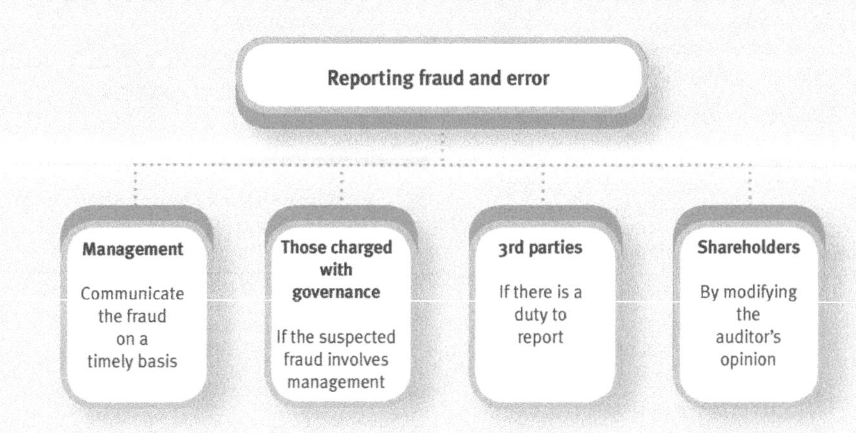
Reporting fraud and error
Management
Communicate the fraud on a timely basis
Those charged with governance
If the suspected fraud involves management
3rd parties
If there is a duty to report
Shareholders
By modifying the auditor's opinion

Auditor liability

Auditors are liable to the client if they fail to comply with the terms of the engagement letter e.g. to deliver and competent and professional service.

For the auditor to be found liable to a third party:

1. A duty of care must exist
   - The auditor must know, or should have known, that the injured party was likely to rely on the financial statements
   - The injured party must have sufficient 'proximity' i.e. he must belong to a class likely to rely on the financial statements
   - The injured party must in fact have so relied
   - The injured party must show that he would have acted differently if the financial statements had shown a less attractive picture.
2. The duty of care must have been breached.
3. Loss must have been suffered as a result of the breach.

Solutions to the negligence problem

- Restrict use of documents to intended use
- Engagement letter and audit report to include disclaimer clause to limit liability
- Screening potential clients
- Take specialist advice
- Respective responsibilities to be communicated and agreed
- Insurance – professional indemnity insurance

- Carry out high quality work
- Take on LLP status
- Set liability cap with client

Expectation gap

The gap that exists between what the public, especially users of financial statements, believe auditors do (or ought to do) and what the auditors actually do.

Potential ways of closing the gap

- Users having a better understanding of the meaning, purposes and limitations of financial statements and the audit report.
- Improved communication between auditors and users of accounts.
- Clarification of the liability for fraud.
- Improved control and education of the auditing profession.

Exam focus

Exam kit questions in this area:

- Margot
- Redback Sports
- Sunshine Hotel Group
- Magnolia Group
- Beyer
- Spaniel

chapter

5

Quality control

In this chapter

- Quality control.

Quality control

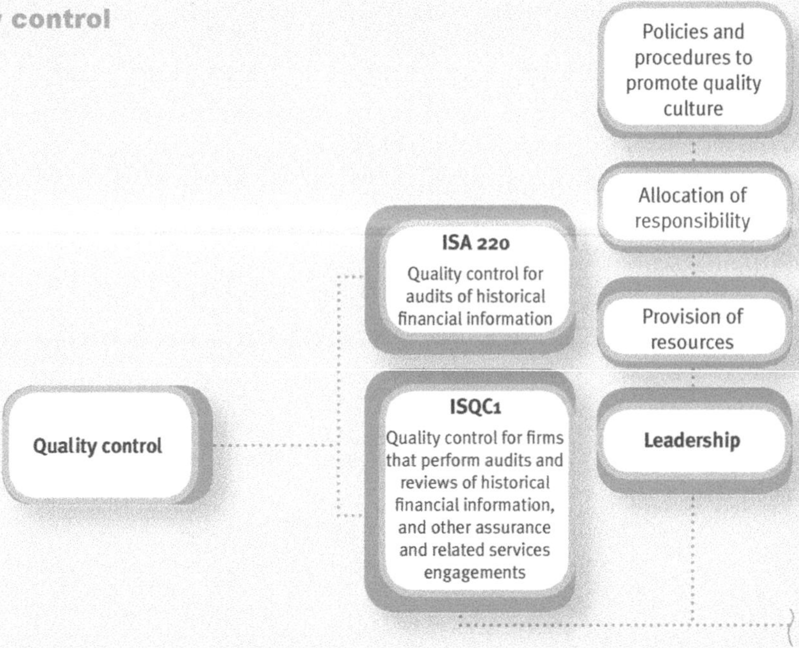

Quality control

ISA 220

Quality control for audits of historical financial information

ISQC1

Quality control for firms that perform audits and reviews of historical financial information, and other assurance and related services engagements

Policies and procedures to promote quality culture

Allocation of responsibility

Provision of resources

Leadership

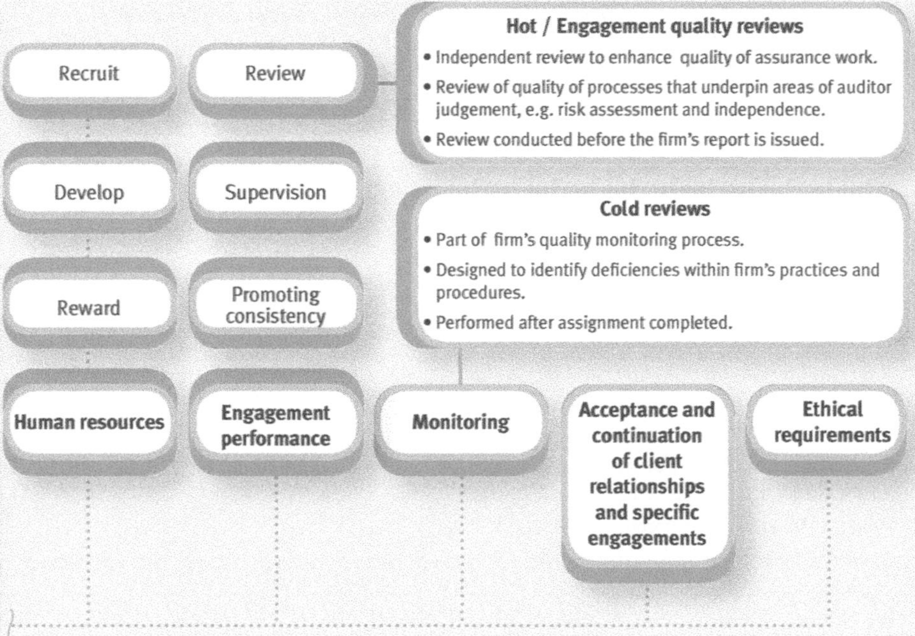

Hot / Engagement quality reviews

- Independent review to enhance quality of assurance work.
- Review of quality of processes that underpin areas of auditor judgement, e.g. risk assessment and independence.
- Review conducted before the firm's report is issued.

Cold reviews

- Part of firm's quality monitoring process.
- Designed to identify deficiencies within firm's practices and procedures.
- Performed after assignment completed.

Recruit

Develop

Reward

Human resources

Review

Supervision

Promoting consistency

Engagement performance

Monitoring

Acceptance and continuation of client relationships and specific engagements

Ethical requirements

Exam focus

A common requirement in the exam is to critically evaluate the audit work already performed on an engagement and identify if the audit has been carried out to the required standard of quality.

To assess the quality of the audit consider the following:

- Have ISAs been followed?
- Has the work been allocated to the appropriate level of staff?
- Has the audit been time pressured?
- Has the appropriate type of evidence been obtained?
- Has the audit been performed in accordance with the audit plan?
- Has the audit been properly supervised and reviewed?

Exam kit questions in this area:

- Eagle Group
- Jansen & Co
- Bradley
- Retriever
- Magnolia Group
- Macau & Co

chapter

6

Practice management

In this chapter

- Tendering.
- Obtaining professional work.
- Engagement letters.

Tendering

Definition

Tendering: the process of quoting a fee for work before it is carried out. This has lead to increased competition within the audit marketplace.

Risks of tendering include: wasted time, setting a low fee, making unrealistic claims/ promised in order to win the contract.

Matters to consider before submitting a tender.

- Resources
- Competences
- Independence
- Risks
- Specialist skills
- Potential for profitability
- Additional services

What goes in a proposal

- The basis of the fee.
- Nature, purpose and legal requirements of an audit.
- Client requirements and how the audit firm will meet them.
- Audit methodology.
- Outline of firm and personnel.
- Assumptions made, e.g. deadlines, geographical coverage, work performed by client.
- Ability of firm to offer other services.

Advantages of tendering	Disadvantages of tendering
• More efficient auditing • Auditing can be a loss leader	• Loss of long-term relationships of clients with auditors • Market choice reduced by increased concentration • Lowballing • Companies may constantly change auditors to reduce costs further

Exam focus

Exam kit questions in this area:

- Weston & Co
- Dragon Group

Obtaining professional work

Obtaining professional work

Advertising and publicity

Fees

ACCA Code of Ethics and Conduct

This material must not:

- Bring disrepute to the ACCA.
- Discredit services offered by others.
- Be misleading.
- Fall short of any advertising codes.

ACCA Code of Ethics and Conduct

- Basis of calculating fees should be pre-agreed and mentioned in the Engagement Letter to avoid contention.
- Fees should be charged bearing in mind factors such as staff seniority, expertise, time spent, apportionable overheads, risk involved.
- Contingency fees should be avoided except customary (e.g. insolvency work).

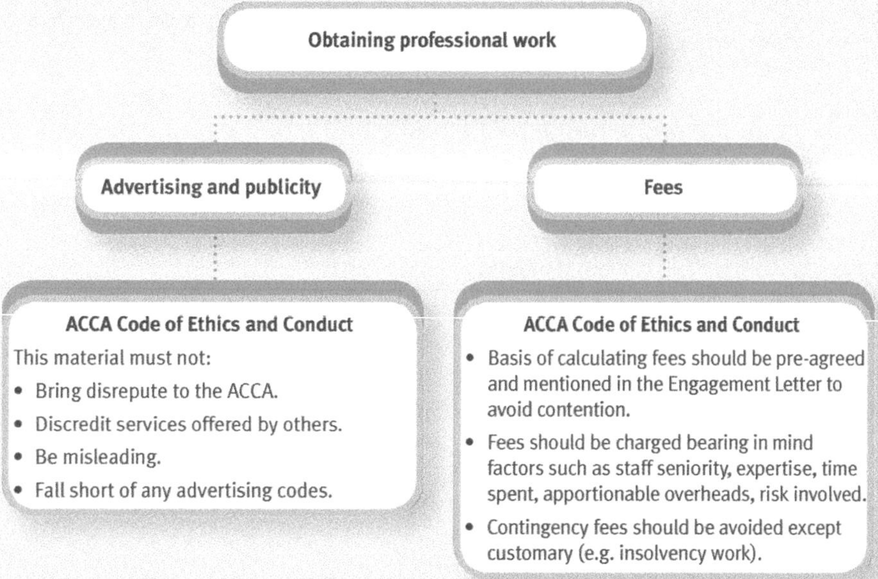

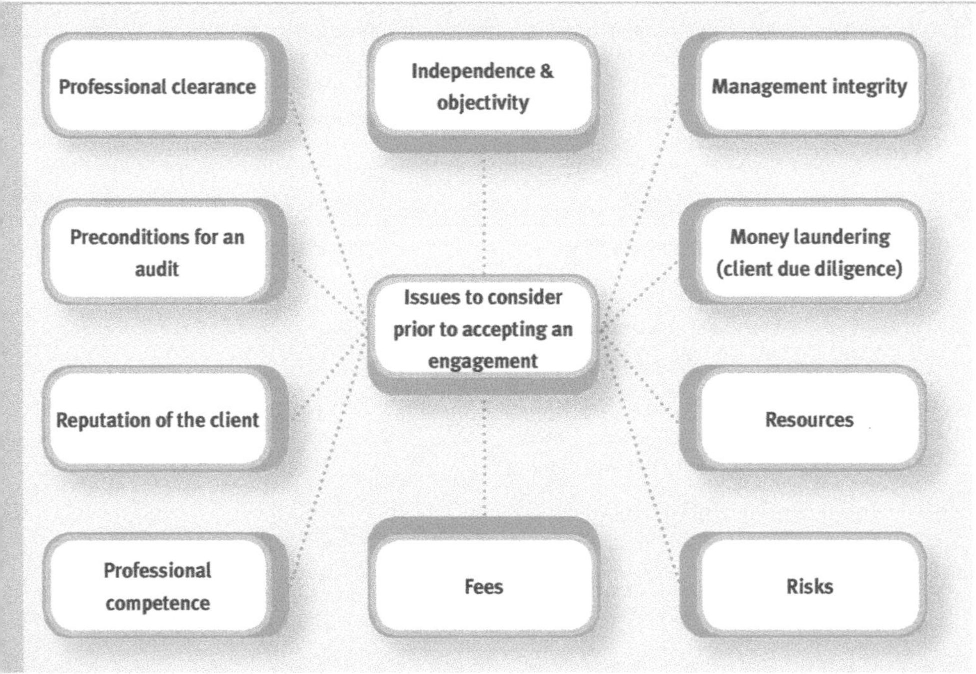

Issues to consider prior to accepting an engagement

- Professional clearance
- Independence & objectivity
- Management integrity
- Preconditions for an audit
- Money laundering (client due diligence)
- Reputation of the client
- Resources
- Professional competence
- Fees
- Risks

Procedures necessary before accepting a new client (where the organisation previously had an auditor. Same principles apply in respect of changes of appointment for all recurring professional work).

Member asked to accept nomination as auditor

Request prospective client's permission to communicate with existing auditor

If permission given, request in writing, all information necessary to decide whether or not to accept nomination

If permission refused, decline nomination

On receipt, existing auditor requests permission of client to communicate with nominee proposed

If permission refused

Proposed nominee declines nomination

If permission given, existing auditor should

Discuss freely with proposed nominee all matters relevant to the appointment

Discuss fully all information by nominee to assist in his decision

Engagement letters

ISA 210 states that the auditor shall agree the terms of the audit engagement with management or those charged with governance, as appropriate.

The terms are recorded in a written audit engagement letter and should include:

- The objective and scope of the audit;
- The responsibilities of the auditor
- The responsibilities of management
- Identification of the applicable financial reporting framework
- The expected form and content of reports to be issued.

Exam focus

- The acceptance of a new client or engagement might be rolled into a wider ranging question regarding ethics.
- In such a question, always consider what steps an auditor must take to ensure that they are acting according to the fundamental principles – it is usually not just about whether previous auditors reply to your request for information!

Exam kit questions in this area:

- Redback Sports
- Bassett Group
- Hawk
- Newman & Co
- Dragon Group

chapter

7

Planning, materiality and assessing the risk of misstatement

In this chapter

- Audit planning.
- Risk assessment.
- Risk assessment procedures.
- Materiality.

Audit planning

Exam focus

Planning is a critical part of the audit process. If it is not carried out with due skill and care, there is a risk that the auditor will be accused of negligence.

In all exams to date there has been one compulsory question involving planning and risk assessment in a range of different scenarios.

ISA 300 Planning an Audit of Financial Statements

In accordance with ISA 300 the auditor should establish an audit strategy and an audit plan. This includes consideration of:

Strategy:

- Scope:
  - engagement characteristics
  - reporting objectives
  - significant engagement factors
  - preliminary activity results
  - the resources needed.
- Timing of when to deploy resources.
- Management, direction and supervision of resources (including meetings, debriefs, reviews etc).

Plan

- Nature, timing and extent of risk assessment procedures.
- Nature, timing and extent of further audit procedures, including:
  - what audit procedures
  - who should do them
  - how much should be done
  - when the work should be done.
- Other necessary procedures.

Risk assessment

In order to comply with ISAs auditors are required to design procedures to reduce audit risk to an acceptable level.

Audit risk is the risk that the auditor offers an inappropriate audit opinion. It is influenced by two further risk categories:

- **Risk of material misstatement**, i.e. the risk that the financial statements are misstated
- **Detection risk**, i.e. the risk that audit procedures fail to detect material misstatement.

Risk of material misstatement is a factor of:

- Inherent risk (i.e. the risk that fraud or error occurs in the first instance)
- Control risk (i.e. the risk that client controls fail to prevent and/or detect fraud and error).

In order to understand the level of inherent and control risk auditors must obtain an understanding the client entity and its environment, in accordance with ISA 315.

This generally includes:

- Relevant industry, regulatory and other external factors
- The nature of the entity, including:
  - its operations
  - its ownership and governance structures
  - the types of investment it makes
  - the way it is structured and financed.
- The entity's selection and application of accounting policies
- The entity's objectives, strategies and related business risks
- The measurement and review of the entity's financial performance
- The internal controls relevant to the audit.

Business Risk

Business risk includes all those factors that threaten a client's ability to meet their strategic objectives, namely profit targets.

These are an important part of inherent risk assessment because they also have a potential impact on the financial statements.

In the exam make sure business risks focus on the impact to the profit or cash flow of the company.

	Audit risk / Risk of material misstatement	Business risk
Major customer in financial difficulty unable to pay their debts.	Receivables may be overstated if bad debts have not been written off.	A bad debt will arise which will reduce profit if written off.
Company purchases goods from overseas.	Purchases may be misstated if the transactions are not translated using an appropriate exchange rate. Payables may be misstated if not revalued using the year end exchange rate.	Purchases may become more expensive if the exchange rate moves in an adverse direction which will reduce profit.
Change in laws and regulations affecting the company	Risk of unrecorded liabilities if the company is not compliant with the new regulations.	The company may have to incur significant cost to become compliant. Fines or penalties may be imposed for non-compliance. This will reduce profit.
Sales have decreased significantly and the company is closing a number of sites.	Asset values may be overstated due to impairment.	Falling sales and reduced capacity will impact profit and cash flow.

Risk assessment procedures

Auditors should

Obtain an understanding of the accounting and internal control systems sufficient to plan the audit and develop an effective audit approach.

Use professional judgement to assess the components of audit risk and to design audit procedures to ensure it is reduced to an acceptably low level.

Risk assessment procedures

- Enquiries of management and others within the entity
- Analytical procedures
- Observation and inspection.

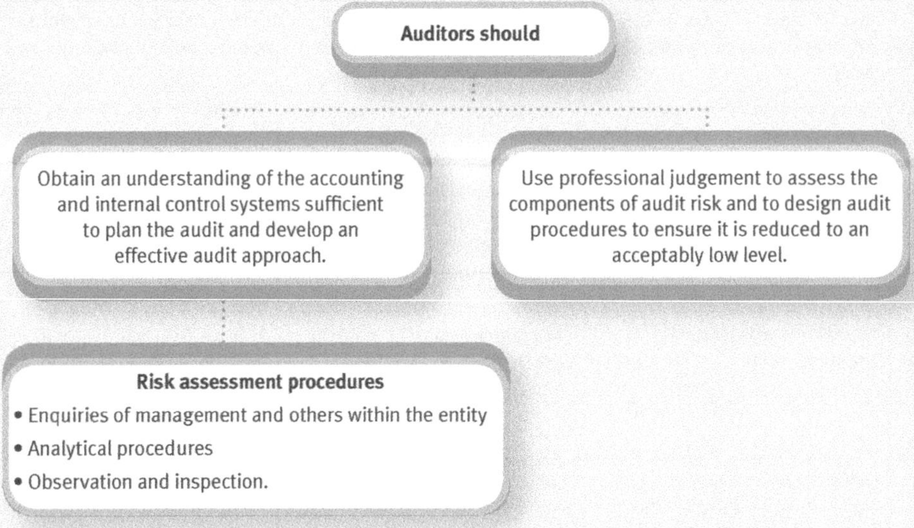

Materiality

ISA 320 Materiality – 'Information is material if its omissions or misstatement could influence the economic decisions of users taken on the basis of the FS'

Materiality should be considered in relation to:

- Financial statements as a whole
- The unique circumstances of the business
- The informational requirements of the users.

Ultimately an area of judgement but indicative guidelines for preliminary assessment are:

Revenue 0.5%

Profit before tax 5%

Total assets 1%

Auditor establishes performance materiality:

- at an amount lower than overall materiality
- to assist with testing samples
- to reduce the risk that misstatement in aggregate is material.

Response to risk assessment

The purpose of performing risk assessment is to allow the auditor to modify their detection risk. This is achieved by manipulating the approach to the audit. Examples of this include:

- Allocating complex/risky areas to suitably experienced and competent staff
- Placing more or less reliance on systems and controls
- Altering the volume of substantive procedures performed
- Changing sample sizes
- Performing more or less substantive analytical procedures
- Consulting external experts on technically complex matters
- Changing the timing, frequency and nature of review procedures.

Professional scepticism

Professional scepticism is defined as: 'An attitude that includes a questioning mind, being alert to conditions which may indicate possible misstatement due to error or fraud, and a critical assessment of audit evidence.'

Professional scepticism requires the auditor to be alert to:

- Audit evidence that contradicts other audit evidence.
- Information that brings into question the reliability of audit evidence.
- Conditions that indicate fraud.
- Circumstances that suggest the need for additional audit procedures.

Exam focus

Exam kit questions in this area:

- Ryder Group
- Margot
- Redback Sports
- Eagle Group
- Bassett Group
- Adams Group
- Sunshine Hotel Group
- Laurel Group
- ZCG
- Vancouver Group
- Dali
- Ted
- Connolly
- Grohl
- CS Group

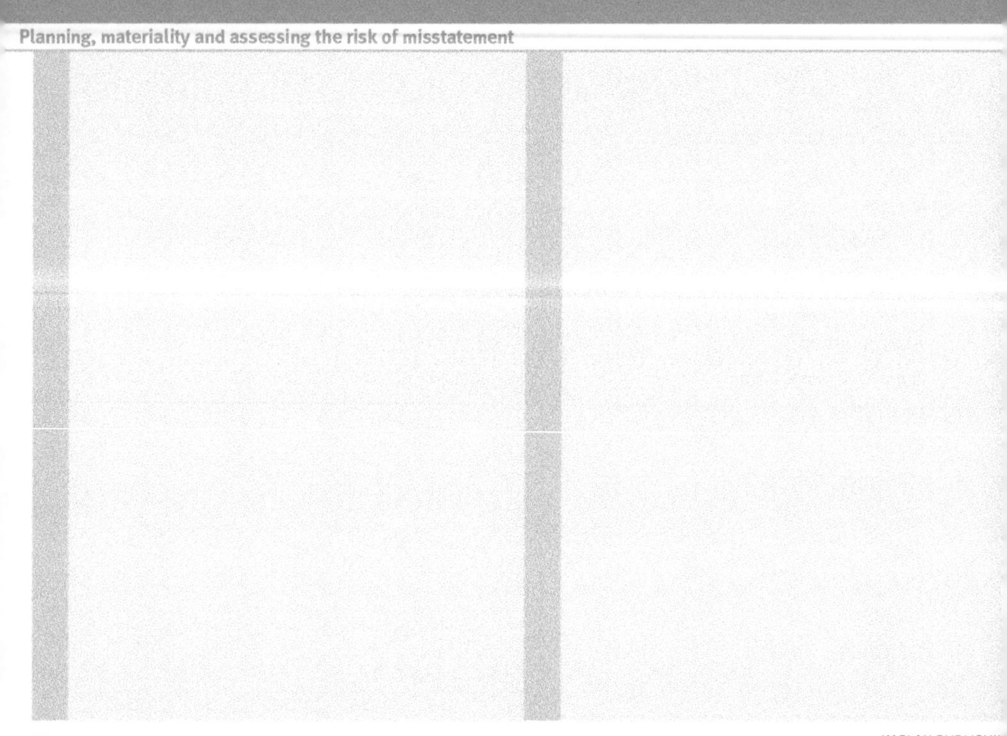

chapter

8

Group and transnational audits

In this chapter

- Treatment of groups.
- Group accounts.
- Regulatory requirements of accounting for groups.
- Joint audits.
- Special considerations.

Treatment of groups

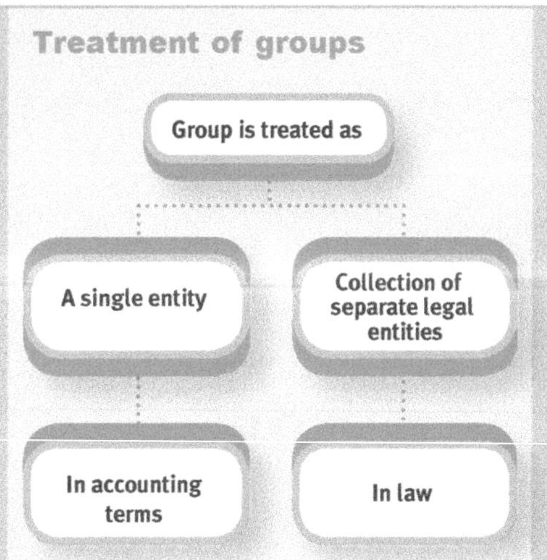

Acceptance as group auditor

In addition to the normal acceptance considerations firms should consider whether to accept the role of group auditor. To assist the decision they must consider:

- Whether sufficient appropriate audit evidence can reasonably be expected to be obtained in relation to the consolidation process and the financial information of the components of the group.
- Where component auditors are involved the engagement partner shall evaluate whether the group engagement team will be able to be involved in the work of the component auditors.
- Whether reliance can be placed on the component auditor's work.
- The materiality of the portion of the group not audited by them.

- Understanding of the group, the components and their environments.
- Any other risks identified which affect the group and its financial statements.

Acceptance as component auditor

The component auditor will consider the following before accepting appointment:

- Whether they are independent of the parent and component companies and can comply with ethical requirements applying to the group audit.
- Whether they possess any special skills necessary to perform the audit of the component and are competent to perform the work.
- Whether they have an understanding of the auditing standards relevant to group audits and can comply with them.
- Whether they have an understanding of the relevant financial reporting framework applicable to the group.
- Whether they can comply with the group audit team instructions including the deadlines.
- Whether they are willing to have the group auditor be involved in their work and evaluate it before relying on it for group audit purposes.

Group accounts

- Group accounts involve consolidation adjustments.
- Relevant accounting standards must be complied with.
- Subsidiaries may be audited by firms other than parent company auditor.

It is the group auditor's responsibility to review the work of component auditors. This is because no part of the audit opinion can be delegated by the group auditor.

Group auditors normally send a consolidation questionnaire to each of the subsidiaries auditors requesting information on:

- accounting policies
- accounting details needed for consolidation.

Problems of auditing foreign subsidiary:

- Geographical location.
- Different accounting policies may be used.
- Language problems.
- Translation of foreign currency amounts required.

Group auditors review of component auditors work includes:

- Review of accounting policies for uniformity.
- Consideration of materiality of amounts involved.
- Considering whether all material areas are covered and whether the work of the component auditors can be relied upon, as well as the competence of the component auditors.

Regulatory requirements of accounting for groups

Auditor should ensure investments are properly classified in accordance with their nature and in line with accounting and legal guidelines – as subsidiaries, associates, JVs or other investments. Main areas of consideration are:

- Accounting policies if not uniform then consolidation adjustments required
- Inter-company transaction and items in transit will require consolidation adjustments
- Accounting periods should be co-terminus (or within three months of each other). Otherwise consolidation adjustments required
- Consider changes in group structure
- Consider loss making subsidiaries and the need for impairments to investments and goodwill

- Intercompany guaranteed loans should be disclosed
- Subsequent events need to consider whether there have been any additions or disposals
- Where there are restrictions on distributions of profit, these should be indicated in the FS

Joint audits

Joint audits arise when the parent company auditors are appointed jointly with the existing auditors of a subsidiary

Advantages:	Disadvantages:
• Improved service through firms different expertise • Improved geographical coverage • Use of two independent firms can provide added assurance to client	• Each joint auditor takes responsibility for the other's shortcomings • May be more expensive • Different firm's audit methods may not be reconciled • Close control of division of work is required

Requirements for effective joint audits:

- Preliminary planning meeting between the two firms to decide on timing, work allocation etc.
- Final meeting to discuss audit issues, conclusions, management letter and joint audit opinion.
- Proper work allocation to avoid dominance.
- Both firms should have adequate professional indemnity insurance.

Special considerations

Subsidiaries in developing countries may not have a fully developed system of accounting and auditing standards. Hence, group auditor can:

- request group directors to adjust financial statements to comply with IFRS Standards
- require the local auditor to conform to ISAs or to perform further audit procedures.

If one or more of subsidiaries has a modified auditor's opinion (regardless of who the auditor was), group auditor should:

- ignore the matter if immaterial at a group level
- modify the group audit opinion if material at a group level.

In accounting terms, a group is a single entity. In legal terms, however, it is a collection of legal entities – which may mean that a component entity may not be a going concern without the support of the group.

The custom is for the directors to give the auditor a comfort/support letter assuring that the group will support the subsidiary – this will be taken by the auditor as valid audit evidence of the going concern basis of the subsidiary's FS.

Exam focus

- At this level, scenarios will likely include a complex element which may involve groups. As such, it is important to be aware of the main accounting and auditing issues involved.

Transnational audits

An audit of financial statements which may be relied upon outside the audited entity's home jurisdiction.

Reliance on these audits might be for purposes of significant lending, investment or regulatory decisions.

The differences between a 'normal' audit, conducted within the boundaries of one set of legal and regulatory requirements, and a transnational audit are largely due to variations in:

- Auditing standards
- Regulation and oversight of auditors
- Financial reporting standards
- Corporate governance requirements.

Exam focus

Exam kit questions in this area:

- Ryder Group
- Eagle Group
- Bassett Group
- Adams Group
- Sunshine Hotel Group
- Laurel Group
- ZCG
- Vancouver Group
- CS Group

chapter

9

Evidence

In this chapter

- Obtaining audit evidence.
- Related party transactions.
- Using the work of an auditor's expert.
- Using the work of an internal audit.
- Outsourcing and the auditor.
- Automated tools and techniques.

Obtaining audit evidence

ISA 500 Audit Evidence, states that ' auditors should obtain SUFFICIENT APPROPRIATE audit evidence to be able to draw reasonable conclusions on which to base the audit opinion'

Sufficient – the necessary quantity must be obtained.

Appropriate – the audit evidence must be of a necessary quality – both relevant and reliable.

SUFFICIENCY – as determined by a number of factors e.g. Materiality of item being examined, auditor's knowledge and judgement.

Relevant – Evidence is required that will enable auditor to draw conclusions on the financial statement assertions.

Reliable – auditor should consider source and its reliability – e.g. written, external and original.

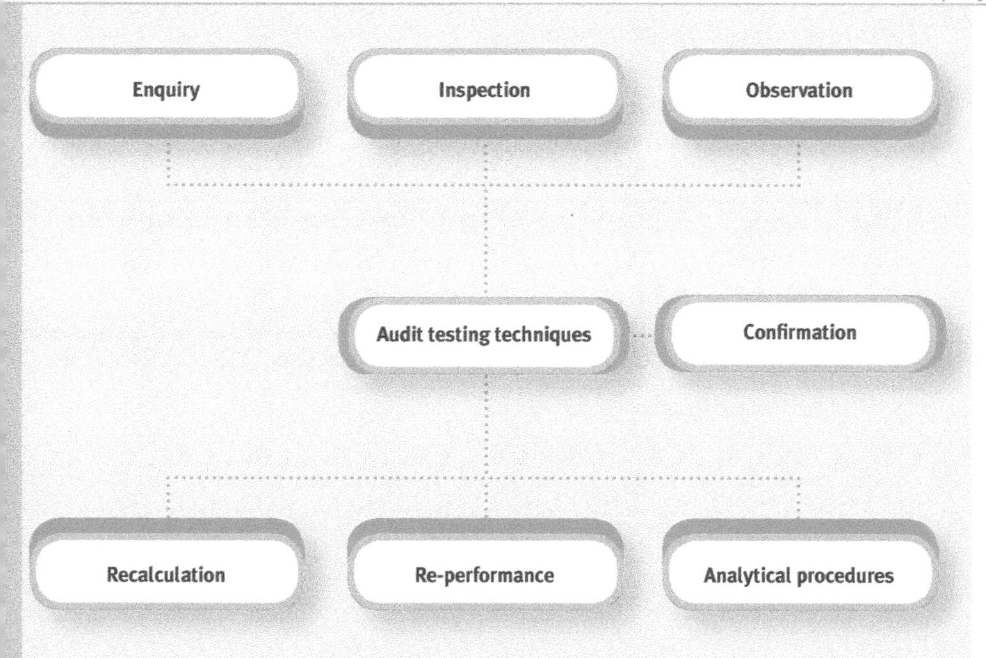
Enquiry
Inspection
Observation
Audit testing techniques
Confirmation
Recalculation
Re-performance
Analytical procedures

Related party transactions (ISA 550)

IAS 24 *Related Party Disclosures:*

- Where control exists, this relationship should be disclosed irrespective whether any transactions have taken place.
- Where transactions have taken place, make disclosure of:

(1) nature of relationship

(2) types of transactions

(3) elements of the transactions necessary for an understanding of the FS.

Parties are related if one has the ability to control or exercise significant influence over the other.

Audit risks with RPTs

- Directors may be reluctant to disclose related party transactions e.g. transactions with family members.
- Transactions may not be easy to identify from the accounting systems.
- Transactions may be concealed in whole, or in part, from auditors for fraudulent purposes.

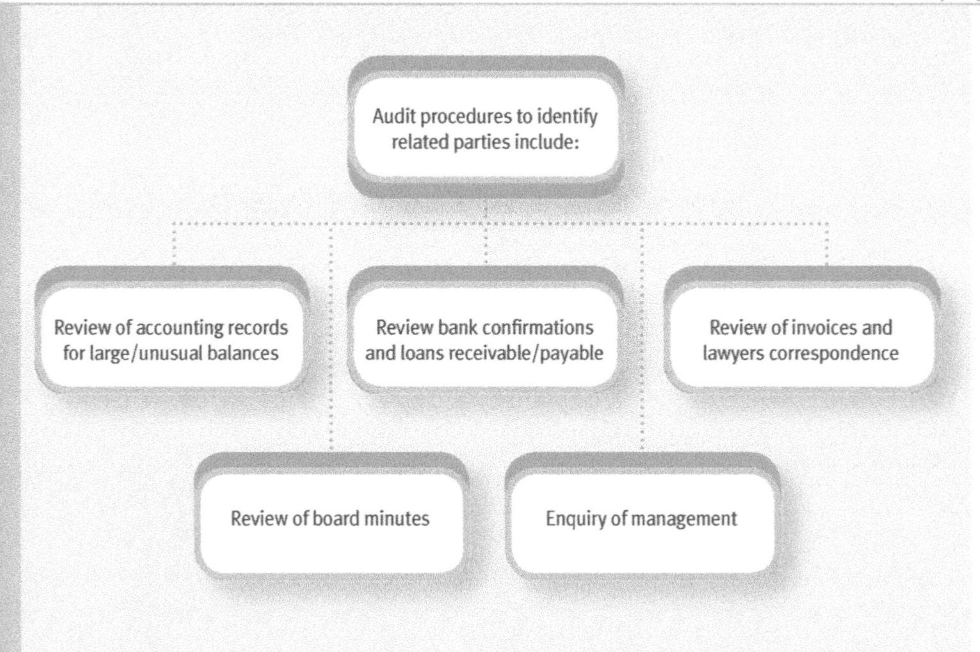
Audit procedures to identify related parties include:
Review of accounting records for large/unusual balances
Review bank confirmations and loans receivable/payable
Review of invoices and lawyers correspondence
Review of board minutes
Enquiry of management

Using the work of an auditor's expert (ISA 620)

Auditor's expert

Person/firm providing specialist skill, knowledge and experience

Auditor must obtain sufficient and appropriate evidence that the work performed by the expert is adequate for audit purposes

1. Agree which expert to use – consider competence, capability and objectivity
2. Agree the nature and scope of the work with the expert
3. Assess the expert's work – consistency of findings with other work, reasonableness of assumptions, source data

Using the work of internal audit (ISA 610)

Before relying on the work of internal audit, the external auditor must assess whether the work produced by the internal auditor is adequate for the purpose of the audit.

1. Evaluate the IA function
2. Evaluate the IA work

IA Function

- Objectivity of IA
- Competence of IA
- Systematic and disciplined approach

IA Work

- Properly planned and performed
- QC procedures in place
- Sufficient appropriate evidence obtained
- Valid conclusions reached

Using internal audit to provide direct assistance

- Internal audit function can provide direct assistance to the external auditor under their supervision and review.
- Cannot be provided where laws and regulations prohibit such assistance.
- The competence and objectivity of the internal auditor must be considered.
- Must not do work which involves significant judgement, a high risk of material misstatement or with which the internal auditor has been involved.
- Planned work must be communicated with those charged with governance.
- Cannot make excessive use of internal auditor.
- Management must not intervene in that work.
- Internal auditors must keep the external auditor's information confidential.
- External auditor will provide direction, supervision and review of the internal auditor's work.
- External auditor should remain alert to the risk that the internal auditor is not objective or competent.

Outsourcing and the auditor

Outsourcing: using an external company (service organisation) to provide a business function or service instead of the organisation doing it in-house.

Implications for external auditors

ISA 402 Audit Considerations Relating to an Entity Using a Service Organisation.

- Obtain an understanding of the service organisation (nature of services provided and relationship with client, materiality of transactions). Obtain understanding through:
  - Inquiries with client
  - Confirmations from the service organisation and their auditors
  - Visits to the service organisation
  - Type 1 or type 2 report from service organisation auditors.
- Design and perform audit procedures responsive to those risks.

  If controls are expected to operate effectively:

  - Obtain a type 2 report if available
  - Perform tests of controls at the service organisation
  - Use another auditor to perform tests of controls.
- Reporting.

  Consider whether sufficient appropriate audit evidence has been obtained, if not, modify the audit opinion.

  The auditor is fully responsible for their opinion, therefore the use of the service organisation or their auditor is not mentioned in the auditor's report.

Automated tools and techniques

Test data	Audit software
Test data is data generated by the auditor which is then processed using the client's computer systems.	Software specially designed for audit purposes.
Put dummy data through the system and make sure the controls within operate as they should. Valid data should be accepted Invalid data should be rejected.	It is used for: Selecting samples. Checking computations and calculations by reperformance. Comparing two or more different files. Performing detailed analytical review.

Data analytics

Data analytics is the science of examining large data sets (big data) with the purpose of drawing conclusions about that information.

Data analytics are a more sophisticated form of computer assisted audit technique.

Benefits

- Allows the auditor to manipulate 100% of the data in a population quickly.
- Can be used throughout the audit to help identify risks, test the controls and as part of substantive procedures.
- Audit quality should increase as sampling risk is reduced.
- As audit quality increases the auditor's liability risk is reduced.
- Audit procedures can be performed more quickly and to a higher standard.

- Audit procedures can be carried out on a continuous basis rather than being focused at the year-end.
- Reporting to the client and users will be more timely.

Exam focus

- The syllabus area on audit evidence is critical to the exam. A common exam question in the past has been scenario based with the requirement to "state the audit evidence you would expect to find".
- You will be expected to be aware of the relative merits of different types of evidence and how far they are reliable. You will also be expected to consider alternative sources.

- The key points covered by the ISAs in this section will provide you with the tools to approach such a question – you will, however, need to apply your knowledge as far as possible to the scenario given!

Exam focus

Exam kit questions in this area:

- Ryder Group
- Margot
- Awdry
- Redback Sports
- Eagle Group
- ZCG
- Osier
- Adder Group
- Francis Group
- Cooper
- Snipe

chapter

10

Completion

In this chapter

- Subsequent events.
- Going concern.
- Overall review.
- Evaluation of misstatements.
- Written representations.

Subsequent events (ISA 560)

Up to the date of the auditor's report	After the date of the auditor's report but before the FS are issued	After the FS are issued
Auditors should peform procedures **designed to obtain sufficient appropriate audit evidence that all events up** to the date of the auditor's report that may require adjustment or disclosure have been identified.	Auditor **has no responsibility** to perform procedures or make enquiry regarding FS after auditor's report date. If auditor becomes aware of amendment should discuss with management and consider implications for auditor's report.	Auditor has **no obligation** to make any inquiry regarding FS. If new information relating to prior to the date of auditor's report comes to light, auditor should consider revision of FS and discuss with management.

Going concern (ISA 570)

Fundamental principle: When **planning** and performing auditing procedures and in **evaluating** the results, the auditor should consider the appropriateness of **management's** use of the going concern assumption in the preparation of the FS.

Management is required to make an assessment of the enterprise's ability to continue for the foreseeable future considering the following factors:

Financial eg

- BS position
- Budgeted negative cash flows
- Maturing debts without realistic prospect of repayment

Operating eg

- Loss of key management without replacement
- Loss of major market

Other eg

- Non-compliance with capital or other statutory requirements

Auditors must review management's going concern assessment, gather sufficient appropriate evidence to confirm/dispel whether a material uncertainty exists and seek management representations regarding future plans. In carrying out evaluation, procedures should include:

- Analysing and discussing latest and budgeted financial information
- Reading board minutes for reference to financial difficulties and future plans
- Review loan agreement terms and determining whether there has been or will likely be any breach

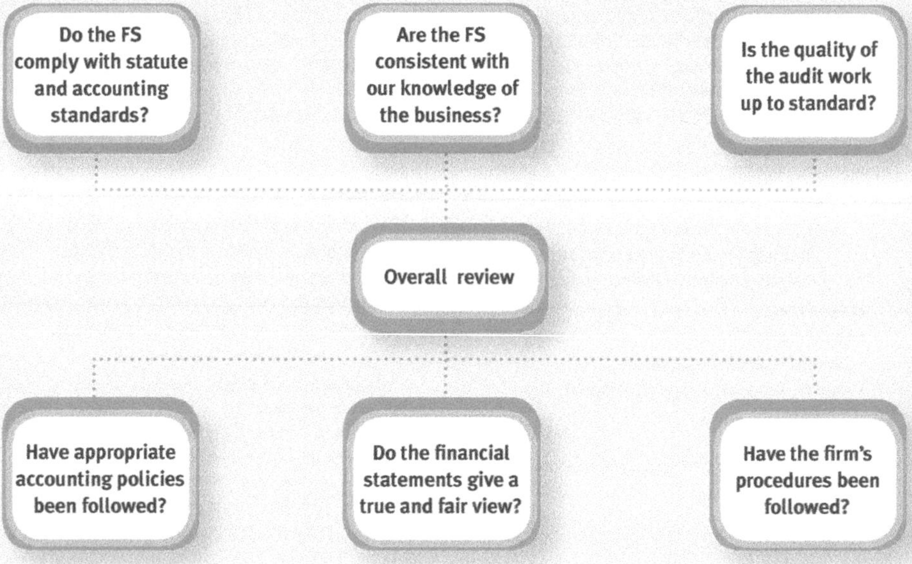

Overall review

- Do the FS comply with statute and accounting standards?
- Are the FS consistent with our knowledge of the business?
- Is the quality of the audit work up to standard?
- Have appropriate accounting policies been followed?
- Do the financial statements give a true and fair view?
- Have the firm's procedures been followed?

Overall review

The reviewer should ask:

- Has the work has been performed in accordance with professional standards and regulatory and legal requirements?
- What significant matters have been raised for further consideration?
- Have appropriate consultations taken place and the resulting conclusions been documented and implemented?
- Is there a need to revise the nature, timing and extent of the work performed?
- Does the work performed support the conclusions reached?
- Is the work appropriately documented?
- Is the evidence obtained sufficient and appropriate to support the auditor's report?
- Have the objectives of the engagement procedures have been achieved?

Evaluation of misstatements (ISA 450)

- All identified errors should be recorded on a working paper set up for the purpose.
- Individually immaterial errors may, in aggregate, amount to a material difference.
- Management should be requested to adjust all identified misstatements.
- All uncorrected misstatements should be communicated to those charged with governance and a description of the implications for the auditor's report, if appropriate.
- If any material misstatements remain unadjusted the auditor would modify the audit opinion.

Written representations (ISA 580)

Key revision points

- Where management make oral representations to auditors during the course of an audit – to avoid misunderstandings and to provide more reliable audit evidence, these representations are documented in a letter.
- The management representations may be the primary source of evidence but they are NOT a substitute for other corroborative evidence that may be available.
- If contradictory evidence is found, further investigation is required.
- Management should be informed of the existence of the letter and be involved in the drafting to avoid conflict and misunderstandings – where management refuses to co-operate in this area, auditor should consider modifying the audit opinion due to a lack of sufficiently reliable evidence.

Matters included in a written representation letter:

General matters

- Management has fulfilled its responsibility for preparing the FS
- Management have provided all relevant information to the auditor

Matters required by other ISAs

- All known and suspected frauds have been communicated to the auditor (ISA 240)
- All instances of non-compliance with laws and regulations have been communicated to the auditor (ISA 250)
- Management believe the effects of uncorrected misstatements are immaterial (ISA 450)

- All related parties and related party disclosures have been disclosed (ISA 550)
- All subsequent events have been communicated to the auditor (ISA 560)
- All going concern issues have been communicated to the auditor (ISA 570)

Specific matters

- Matters involving management judgement or intentions of management

Exam focus

Exam kit questions in this area:

- Lifeson
- Kilmister
- Daley
- Coram & Co
- Brearley & Co
- Magnolia Group
- Basking
- Osier
- Rocket
- Boston
- Darren
- Adder Group
- Francis Group
- Cooper
- Poodle Group
- Snipe
- Macau & Co

chapter

11

Reporting

In this chapter

- The auditors' report.
- Reporting to those charged with governance.
- Communicating deficiencies in internal control.

The auditors' report

INT Syllabus	UK syllabus
• Title • Addressee • Auditor's opinion • Basis for opinion • Material uncertainty related to going concern (if applicable) • Emphasis of matter (if applicable) • Key audit matters (Listed companies) • Other information • Responsibilities of management • Auditor's responsibilities • Report on other legal and regulatory requirements • Other matter (if applicable) • Signature • Auditor's address • Date	• Title • Addressee • Auditor's opinion • Basis for opinion • Conclusions relating to going concern / Material uncertainty related to going concern (if applicable) • Emphasis of matter (if applicable) • Key audit matters, our application of materiality, an overview of the scope of our audit (Listed companies) • Other information • Opinion on other matters prescribed by the Companies Act 2006 • Matters on which we are required to report by exception • Responsibilities of directors • Auditor's responsibilities • Other matter (if applicable) • Signature • Auditor's address • Date

Unmodified opinion

- If the auditor believes the financial statements to be 'true and fair' they issue an unmodified auditor's opinion.

Modifications that affect the opinion

The opinion should be modified under the following circumstances:

- the financial statements are **NOT** free from material misstatement; or
- the auditor was unable to obtain sufficient appropriate evidence.

The wording of the opinion then depends upon whether the misstatement is:

- material but not pervasive (i.e. isolated to certain elements of the financial statements); or
- material and pervasive (i.e. infiltrates so much of the financial statements that they are unreliable as a whole).

	Material	Material & Pervasive
Financial statements contain material misstatement	Qualified opinion (i.e. "except for")	Adverse opinion (i.e. "do not show a true and fair view")
Unable to obtain sufficient appropriate evidence	Qualified opinion (i.e. "except for")	Disclaimer of opinion (i.e. "we do not express an opinion")

Other audit reporting implications

Situation	Refer to in:	Impact on opinion
Going concern uncertainties adequately disclosed	Material uncertainty related to going concern	Unmodified
Inconsistencies between the other information and the financial statements	Other information	Unmodified
Matters of fundamental importance disclosed in the financial statements to be brought to the attention of the users	Emphasis of matter paragraph	Unmodified
Matters relating to the auditor's responsibilities, the audit or auditor's report to be explained further to the users	Other matter paragraph	Unmodified
Explanation of why a modified opinion is being given	Basis for opinion	Modified

UK syllabus only: Conclusions related to going concern

If there are no going concern issues to report, (i.e. the basis of preparation is appropriate and no disclosures are required), the auditor must make a statement to this effect in the auditor's report.

Reporting to those charged with governance

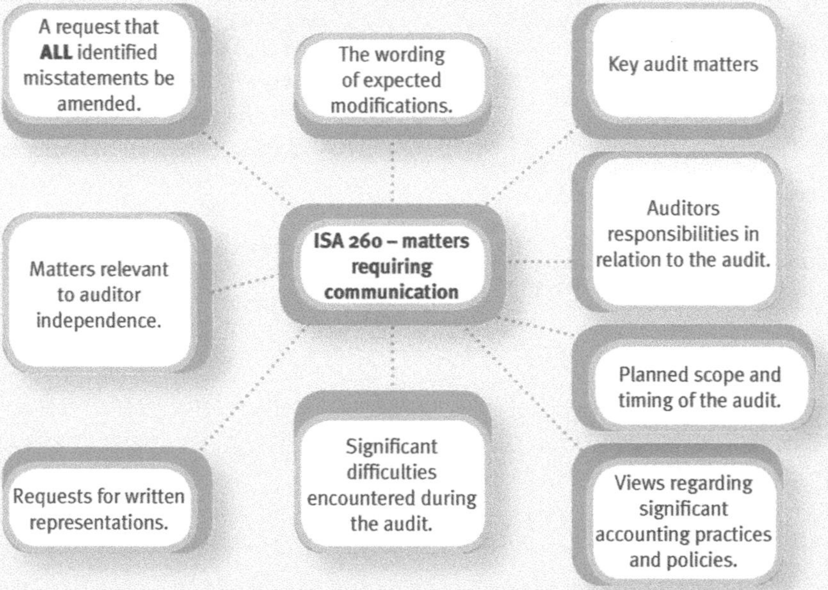

ISA 260 – matters requiring communication

- A request that **ALL** identified misstatements be amended.
- The wording of expected modifications.
- Key audit matters
- Matters relevant to auditor independence.
- Auditors responsibilities in relation to the audit.
- Planned scope and timing of the audit.
- Requests for written representations.
- Significant difficulties encountered during the audit.
- Views regarding significant accounting practices and policies.

Communicating deficiencies in internal control

Auditors are required to communicate identified deficiencies in internal control on a timely basis in accordance with ISA 265.

When deciding who to report to the auditor should determine whether the deficiencies, either individually or in aggregate, are significant.

If necessary the auditor should communicate deficiencies in internal control to management.

Significant deficiencies in internal control must be communicated to those charged with governance in writing. The communication should include:

- A description of the deficiency
- An explanation of their potential effects
- Sufficient information to understand the context of the communication in relation to the audit process.

Commonly, the additional reports required by ISAs 260 and 265 are referred to as "Management Letters" or "Findings from the Audit Letters."

Exam focus

- The form and content of the auditor's report is a highly examinable area – after all, it is the final deliverable after the planning and performance of the audit!
- Be prepared to consider if an item is material, how it affects the interpretation of the reader and, therefore whether modification to the auditor's report is required.
- You may have to critically appraise a draft report. This requires thought about the order of the paragraphs, the style of the wording used, as well as whether the opinion suggested is appropriate.

Exam focus

Exam kit questions in this area:

- Lifeson
- Kilmister
- Daley
- Coram & Co
- Brearley & Co
- Magnolia Group
- Basking
- Osier
- Rocket
- Boston
- Darren
- Adder Group
- Francis Group
- Cooper
- Poodle Group
- Snipe
- Macau & Co

chapter

12

Audit-related services

In this chapter

- Audit related services.

Assurance engagements	Agreed-upon procedures
• Engagements to review the financial statements of companies that do not have to be audited (eg, small companies). • Interim financial information. • Due diligence assignments. • PFI engagements. • Environmental/social reporting.	• Forensic audits – Fraud investigation. – Verifying insurance claims. • Due diligence.

Audit related services

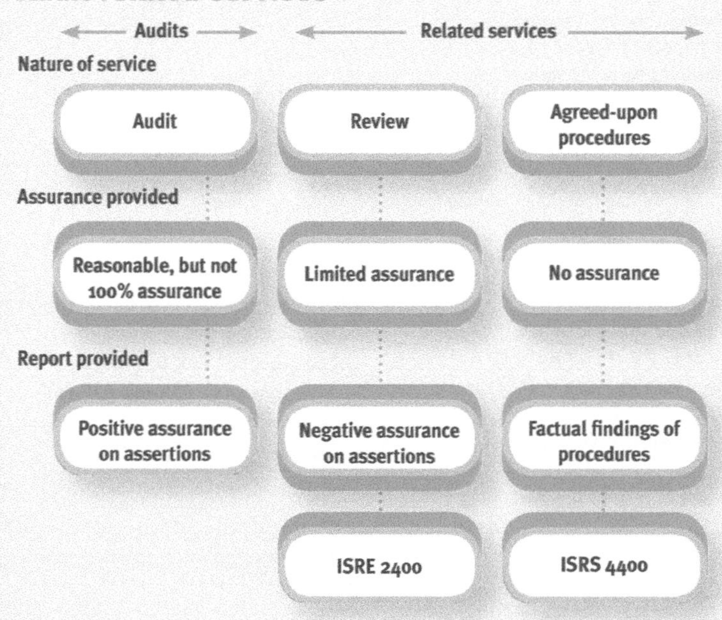

Levels of assurance

The International Framework for Assurance Engagements permits only two types of assurance engagement to be performed:

- Reasonable assurance: the reporting accountant concludes that the subject matter conforms in all material respects with identified suitable criteria. Reports express positive assurance, i.e. giving an opinion that the subject matter is (or is not) free from material misstatement.
- Limited assurance: the reporting accountant concludes that the subject matter is plausible in the circumstances. Reports express negative assurance, i.e. that procedures have not identified any material misstatement regarding the subject matter.

Reporting

- Title
- Addressee
- Identification and description of the subject matter
- Identification of the criteria
- Description of any significant, inherent limitations
- Restriction on the use of the report to specific users
- Statement of responsibilities of the responsible party and practitioner
- Statement that the engagement was performed in accordance with professional standards
- Summary of the work performed
- Practitioner's conclusion
- Date
- Name of the firm or practitioner and location

chapter

13

Review of interim financial information

In this chapter

- Interim financial information.

Interim financial information

A complete or condensed set of financial statements for a period shorter than a financial year.

Objective of a review of interim financial information

To enable the auditor to express a conclusion whether, on the basis of the review, anything has come to the auditor's attention that causes the auditor to believe that the interim financial information is not prepared, in all material respects, in accordance with an applicable financial reporting framework.

Principles of the review

- Comply with the ethical requirements
- Comply with *ISRE 2410 Review of Interim Financial Information Performed by the Independent Auditor of the Entity.*
- Implement appropriate quality control procedures.
- Consider whether the engagement should be accepted.
- Agree the terms of engagement.
- Plan the engagement so that it will be performed effectively including:
  - Applying professional scepticism.
  - Obtaining an understanding of the subject matter.
  - Assessing the suitability of the criteria to evaluate the subject matter.
  - Consideration of materiality and engagement risk.
- Obtain sufficient appropriate evidence on which to base the conclusion.
- Consider subsequent events.
- Document matters significant in providing evidence that supports the engagement report.

- Provide a clear written expression of their conclusion about the subject matter information.

Procedures

- Enquiries of relevant parties (usually management).
- Analytical procedures.
- Other review procedures as necessary to obtain sufficient appropriate evidence
- Written representations from management

Exam focus

Exam kit questions in this area:

- Squire

chapter

14

Prospective financial information

In this chapter

- Prospective financial information.
- Procedures.

Prospective financial information

A reporting accountant may be asked to provide an opinion on prospective (future) financial information in the form of a forecast and/ or projection (ISAE 3400 is the authoritative standard in this area).

PFI = Financial information based on assumptions about events that may occur in the future and possible actions by the entity.

FORECAST= PFI based on management expectations (best-estimate assumptions).

PROJECTION= PFI based on hypothetical assumptions about future events that may or may not take place or based on a combination of best-estimate and hypothetical assumptions.

Prior to **ACCEPTANCE** of a PFI engagement, the auditor must consider:

- The intended users.
- Whether the information will be for general or limited distribution.
- The nature of assumptions: best estimate or hypothetical?
- Elements to be included and period covered.

Procedures

- Cast the forecast to verify arithmetical accuracy.
- Compare previous forecasts with actual results to assess the ability of the preparer.
- Compare accounting policies used in the financial statements to those used in the forecast to ensure consistency.
- Agree opening cash figure to cash book (if already within the forecast period).
- Calculate key ratios and trends to assess reasonableness of the forecast figures.
- Enquire of management where there are unusual movements expected.
- Enquire of management of their plans for the forecast period and ensure these are reflected in the figures.
- Compare forecast with management accounts for prior year to assess reasonableness of figures and identify any missing items.
- Compare forecast to management accounts for period to date to see if the figures are in line.
- Review forecast for any items which are to be discontinued and ensure they are not included.
- Review forecast for any new costs/ incomes that should be included that weren't present previously.
- Compare trends with industry expectations to assess reasonableness.
- Obtain written representation from management that they believe the assumptions are reasonable.
- Inspect the forecast for any new loans

and interest to ensure they have been included.

Make sure your procedures are relevant to the type of forecast being examined. Cash flow forecasts should focus on forecast receipts and payments on a cash basis.

Exam focus

Profit forecasts should focus on forecast incomes and expenditures on an accruals basis.

Exam kit questions in this area:

- Jansen & Co
- Vizsla
- Rope
- Waters
- Hawk

chapter

15

Due diligence

In this chapter

- Due diligence.

Due diligence

Due diligence involves gathering information for a client on a potential acquisition. The aim is to reduce the risk of making a bad investment.

Consider what information will impact the client's decision to go ahead with the acquisition or what price to pay. Obtain information to suggest whether this is a good or bad investment.

Information required:

- Financial statements
- Forecasts and budgets
- Details of contracts and agreements
- Industry comparisons
- Details of outstanding litigation
- Details of tax investigations
- Details of management contracts
- Factors affecting asset values
- Completeness of liabilities
- Retention of staff
- Quality issues
- Reputational issues
- Likely synergies

Benefits of due diligence

- **D**ecrease management time assessing acquisition
- **I**dentification of operational issues and risks
- **L**iabilities evaluated and identified
- **I**dentify assets not capitalised
- **G**ather information
- **E**nhance credibility of the investment decision
- Pla**N**ning the acquisition
- **C**laims made by vendor substantiated
- **E**valuation of post-acquisition synergies

Exam kit questions in this area:

- Cheetah
- Sanzio
- Baltimore
- Jacob

chapter

16

Forensic audits

In this chapter

- Forensic accounting.
- Applications of forensic accounting.

Forensic accounting

Definition

Forensic accounting is a specialist branch of the profession carried out by forensic accountants and encompassing forensic auditing and investigation.

Planning

- Clarify the objectives and deadline for the engagement.
- Enquire whether the insurance company has been contacted.
- Scrutinise the insurance policy to ensure cover is in place.
- Consider the resources and skills required.
- Confirm with the client that full access to information will be allowed.
- Confirm the output of the investigation.
- Confirm whether you will be required as an expert witness.

Procedures

- Inspection of documents.
- Enquiries of management and staff.
- Analytical procedures.
- Computer assisted audit techniques.
- Tests of controls.

Report

- Summary of the procedures performed.
- Summary of results of procedures.
- Conclusion regarding losses.
- Recommendations to prevent future problems.

Applications of forensic accounting

Application	Examples	Type of work performed
Fraud investigations	Employee embezzlement of company funds, tax evasion, insider dealing.	Funds tracing, asset identification and recovery, forensic intelligence gathering, due diligence reviews, interviews, detailed review of documentary evidence.
Insurance claims	Business interruptions, property losses, motor vehicle incidents, personal liability claims, cases of medical malpractice, wrongful dismissal.	Detailed review of the policy from either an insured or insurer's perspective to investigate coverage issues, identification of appropriate method of calculating the loss, quantification of losses.
Professional negligence	Loss suffered as a result of placing reliance on professional adviser.	Advising on merits of a case in regards to liability, quantifying losses.
Shareholder, partnership and matrimonial disputes	Determination of funds to be included in settlements, as benefits or distributions.	Detailed analysis of numerous years accounting records to quantify the issues in dispute, tracing, locating and evaluation of assets.

Exam focus

- A question on forensic auditing would allow many areas of knowledge to be tested outside of the 'standard' audit scenario.
- Approach any question on forensic auditing with an open mind, consider what the question is asking for and address the requirements – **do not** automatically assume it is related to finding or investigating a fraud!

Exam focus

Exam kit questions in this area:

- Beyer
- Lark & Co
- Retriever

chapter

17

Audit of social, environmental and integrated reporting

In this chapter

- Social and environmental reporting.
- Environmental impact on FS.

Social and environmental reporting

Many companies now publish social and environmental data in their annual reports.

Assurance reports may be attached to this information to increase the credibility of the information.

SER reports detail key performance indicators management consider important to the company.

Social and environmental matters include:

- Tonnes of waste sent to landfill
- Water usage
- Electricity usage
- CO_2 emissions
- $ donated to charity
- Number of staff volunteer days
- Number of serious accidents in the workplace

Planning the engagement

- Understand and agree the scope of the engagement.
- Obtain an understanding of the entity.
- Agree the KPIs over which assurance is to be provided.
- Consider the appropriateness of the KPIs chosen.
- Identify the evidence that should be available.
- Consider the potential for manipulation of each KPI.

Measurement difficulties

- Deciding which KPIs on which to report
- KPIs may not be specific enough to measure accurately.
- The concepts involved may lack precise definition.
- Systems and controls may not be in place to capture the information reliably.

Reporting difficulties

- Accountants may lack the specific skills and experience needed.
- Significant subjectivity of the subject matter.
- Evidence may not be sufficient or appropriate for the purposes of providing assurance.
- Potential for manipulation to achieve the desired result.

Environmental impact on FS

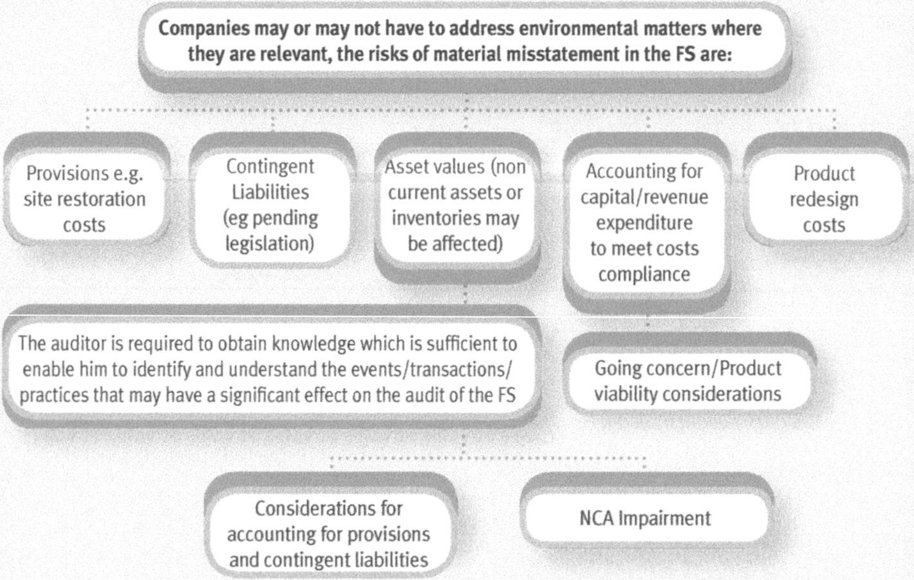

Companies may or may not have to address environmental matters where they are relevant, the risks of material misstatement in the FS are:

- Provisions e.g. site restoration costs
- Contingent Liabilities (eg pending legislation)
- Asset values (non current assets or inventories may be affected)
- Accounting for capital/revenue expenditure to meet costs compliance
- Product redesign costs

The auditor is required to obtain knowledge which is sufficient to enable him to identify and understand the events/transactions/ practices that may have a significant effect on the audit of the FS

Going concern/Product viability considerations

- Considerations for accounting for provisions and contingent liabilities
- NCA Impairment

Exam focus

Exam kit questions in this area:

- Moosewood Hospital
- Newman & Co

chapter

18

INT SYLLABUS ONLY: Audit of performance information in the public sector

In this chapter

- Performance audits and performance information.
- Reporting.

Performance audits and performance information

Performance audits provide assurance regarding the effective functioning of the organisation's operations.

Performance information is published by an organisation to highlight achievement of their objectives. Performance information is in the form of KPIs.

Planning an audit of performance information

- Obtain an understanding of the information to be audited.
- Enquire of management of how the information is collected and recorded.
- Determine an appropriate materiality level.
- Examine the systems and controls for recording the information.

Audit procedures

- Inspection of supporting documentation.
- Enquiries of management and staff.
- Perform analytical procedures.
- Recalculate the figures to verify arithmetical accuracy.
- Obtain written representations from management regarding accuracy and completeness.

Potential problems

As with any KPI, problems may be encountered with:

- Measuring the information in the first instance.
- Subjectivity of definition.

Reporting

An assurance report for performance information may provide reasonable assurance or limited assurance depending on the requirements of the client.

Exam focus

Exam kit questions in this area:

- Kandinsky

chapter

19

UK SYLLABUS ONLY:

Auditing aspects of insolvency

In this chapter

- Voluntary liquidation.
- Compulsory liquidation.
- Administration.
- Alternative to winding up.
- Fraudulent and wrongful trading.

Voluntary liquidation

Liquidation is the process of terminating a company. The assets of the company are physically liquidated to pay off company creditors and equity holders.

There are two forms of voluntary liquidation

- a members' voluntary liquidation (used when a company is solvent)
- a creditors' voluntary liquidation (used when a company is insolvent).

Procedures

Members' VL:

- members pass resolution
- declaration of solvency
- appointment of insolvency practitioner
- final report issued
- company dissolved.

Creditors' VL:

- members pass resolution
- appointment of insolvency practitioner
- final report issued
- company dissolved.

Compulsory liquidation

Companies may be obliged to liquidate if a winding up order is presented to a court, usually by a creditor or member. A petition may be made because:

- the company is unable to pay its debts or
- it is just and equitable to do so.

Procedures

- official receiver obtains consent of creditors
- appointment of insolvency practitioner and liquidation committee
- final report issued
- company dissolved.

Liquidators in a compulsory liquidation must pay debts in the following order:

- fixed charge holders
- liquidation expenses, liquidator's remuneration
- preferential creditors, including wages and accrued holiday pay
- floating charge holders (subject to prescribed part)
- unsecured creditors
- deferred debts, including dividends declared but not paid and accrued interest
- members.

Administration

This is when an insolvency practitioner is appointed to manage the affairs of a business under the Enterprise Act 2002. It is often used as an alternative to liquidation with a view to:

- rescuing a company
- achieving the best result for creditors
- realising property to pay off secured creditors.

Consequences

Administrators take over control of the management of the company. Their powers include:

- removal/appointment of directors
- calling meetings of creditors/members
- making payments to secured or preferential creditors
- making payments to unsecured creditors
- presenting or defending a petition to liquidate the company.

In administration certain protections are afforded to a company:

- the rights of creditors to enforce security over the company's assets are suspended
- petitions for liquidation are dismissed
- no resolutions to wind up the company may be passed
- the directors continue in office, although their powers are suspended.

Advantage of administration

- Provides time to develop survival plan.
- Shareholders are less likely to lose their investment.
- Creditors are more likey to be paid.

Alternative to winding up

Individual Voluntary Arrangements (IVAs)

- available to individuals, sole traders and partnerships
- helps reach a compromise with creditors with the aim of avoiding closure
- usually facilitates lower payments of debt over an extended period, usually five years
- once a proposal is submitted to the courts creditors may no longer take action against the individual (referred to as a moratorium on actions)
- a creditors meeting must be held within fourteen days of the order
- the creditors may accept the proposals with a 75% majority (by value of creditors present) vote.

Reconstructions

Companies in difficulty could survive by through growth and diversification but, in the circumstances, would find it difficult to attract investment.

Various mechanisms of the Companies Act 2006 enable companies to reconstruct their balance sheet to make them more attractive to investment. Permitted reconstructions include:

- writing off unpaid share capital
- writing off share capital not represented by available assets
- writing off paid up share capital in excess of requirements
- writing off debenture interest arrears
- replacing existing debentures with a lower interest debenture
- writing off preference dividend arrears
- writing off amounts owing to trade creditors.

Fraudulent and wrongful trading

Fraudulent trading (a criminal offence) is where a company carries on a business with the **intention of defrauding creditors**.

Wrongful trading (a civil offence) is when the director(s) of a company knew or ought to have concluded that there was **no reasonable prospect of avoiding insolvent liquidation**.

A company is **insolvent** if:

- its liabilities exceed its assets
- it is failing to discharge its debts as they fall due.

Exam focus

Exam kit questions in this area:

- Krupt
- Kandinsky
- Hunt & Co
- Butler

References

The Board (2019) *IAS 24 Related Party Disclosures*. London: IFRS Foundation.

Index

A

B

C

D

E

F

G

H

I

J

L

M

N

O

P

Q

R